636

Do Scientists Care About Animal Welfare?

Eve Hartman and Wendy Meshbesher

www.raintreepublishers.co.uk
Visit our website to find out
more information about
Raintree books.

To order:
☎ Phone 0845 6044371
🖨 Fax +44 (0) 1865 312263
🖳 Email myorders@raintreepublishers.co.uk

Customers from outside the UK please telephone +44 1865 312262

Raintree is an imprint of Capstone Global Library Limited,
a company incorporated in England and Wales having its
registered office at 7 Pilgrim Street, London, EC4V 6LB –
Registered company number: 6695582

Edited by Adam Miller, Andrew Farrow, and
  Adrian Vigliano
Designed by Philippa Jenkins
Original illustrations © Capstone Global Library
  Limited 2012
Illustrated by Terry Pastor / www.theartagency.co.uk
Picture research by Mica Brancic
Originated by Capstone Global Library Ltd
Printed and bound in China by CTPS

ISBN 978 1 406 23383 4 (hardback)
15 14 13 12
10 9 8 7 6 5 4 3 2

British Library Cataloguing in Publication Data
Hartman, Eve.
Do scientists care about animal welfare?. -- (Sci-hi)
636'.0832-dc22
A full catalogue record for this book is available from the
British Library.

Acknowledgments
The author and publishers are grateful to the following
for permission to reproduce copyright material: Corbis
pp. 13 (epa/© Shamshahrin Shamsudin), 19 top (Miles
Brothers), 20 (ZUMA/© Nancy Kaszerman), 21 (Visuals
Unlimited/© Nigel Cattlin), 22 (© Dave Blackey/All
Canada Photos), 24 (© William Campbell), 27 (epa/©
Jo Prichard), 28 (© Hulton-Deutsch Collection), 29 (epa/©
Julian Smith), 30 (© Brant Ward/San Francisco Chronicle),
32 (© John Carnemolla), 33 (© ColorBlind Images/Blend
Images), 34 right (epa/© Tannen Maury); Digitial Frog p.
15; Getty Images p. 34 left (National Geographic/David
Doubilet); Reuters p. 26 (Tim Wimborne); Science Photo
Library p. 11 (Sam Ogden); Shutterstock pp. 4 (©
Photosbyjohn), 7 (© Floris Slooff), 12 (© Aksenova
Natalya), 17 (© Randy Rimland), 23 (© Loyish),
25 (© Guentermanaus), 35 (© PBorowka), 38 (© Oleg
Znamenskiy), 39 (© Armin Rose), 41 (© Tyler Olson),
19 bottom (© Willem Tims), 37 bottom (© Oleksandr
Kalinichenko), 37 top (© Krzysztof Odziomek), contents
page bot (© Randy Rimland), contents page top
(© Floris Slooff). All background design feature pictures
courtesy of Shutterstock.

Main cover photograph of Rhesus monkeys reproduced
with permission of Alamy (© PHOTOTAKE Inc./Richard T.
Nowitz); inset cover photograph of a white mouse sitting
on a grey background reproduced with permission of
Shutterstock (© Narcisse).

The publisher would like to thank literary consultant
Nancy Harris and content consultant Ann Fullick for their
assistance in the preparation of this book.

Every effort has been made to contact copyright holders
of material reproduced in this book. Any omissions will
be rectified in subsequent printings if notice is given to
the publisher.

Contents

Why is the mouse called a mini human?

Find out on page 6!

Should unwanted pets be used for animal testing?

Turn to page 17 to find out!

Some words are shown in bold, **like this**. These words are explained in the glossary. You will find important information and definitions underlined, <u>like this</u>.

ANIMAL WELFARE

Scientists affect **animal welfare** in many ways. Some scientists observe animals in nature or conduct experiments on animals in laboratories. **Veterinarians** help care for animals. Scientists who study animals might work for the government, a university, or a charity. The work of scientists sometimes promotes animal welfare, while sometimes it raises conflicts. As you will discover, the conflicts between science and animal welfare are often not easy to resolve.

We share Earth with a huge variety of animals, including livestock, wildlife, and pets.

WELFARE VERSUS RIGHTS

People use the terms animal welfare and **animal rights** in different ways. In this book, we define animal welfare as the well-being of animals. Animal rights is the idea that animals have rights, just as humans do.

Issues of animal rights are often very controversial. Some people argue that animals have the same rights as humans. They believe we should never kill or use an animal for food or experiments. Others argue that animals should never be treated cruelly, but that human needs should always come first.

What is an animal?

When people discuss animal welfare, they usually think about large, familiar animals. But people often use the word "animal" in different ways. As defined in science, the animal kingdom includes all sorts of species, or types of living things. Not all animals are large or have friendly faces. Insects are animals. So are spiders, worms, snails, and sea sponges.

All animals fill roles in nature, but sometimes these roles can be harmful to humans or other animals. Grasshoppers and whiteflies are farm pests. Mosquitoes and fleas can bite and spread disease. Flukes, a kind of worm, are parasites. They live inside the bodies of larger animals and feed on them. Most people do not care about the welfare of flukes!

ANIMAL TESTING

Before a new food or drug is approved for human use, scientists often test it on animals. They might also use animals to test a new surgical technique, test an artificial limb, or investigate how body systems work. Laws and practices are designed to protect the welfare of test animals. Many scientists argue that these laws and practices are appropriate, and that animal testing is useful and necessary.

MEET THE MINI HUMAN

Why is animal testing useful? The reason is that the bodies of some animals work much like the human body.

The mouse has been called a "mini human". Look at the diagram of mouse **anatomy**. A mouse has a heart, a stomach, lungs, intestines, and other organs that humans have. Many body processes that happen in mice are similar to processes that happen in the bodies of humans.

Mice are small, and they require only a little food. They are easy to handle, raise, and, breed. For all of these reasons, mice are the most common animal used for food and drug testing.

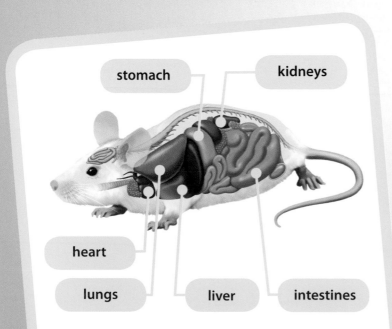

stomach

kidneys

heart

lungs

liver

intestines

Mice, like this one, are bred to be used in labs. They are often albino (white with pink eyes).

THE SCIENTIFIC METHOD

The **scientific method** is the process that scientists use to draw conclusions about the natural world. It involves forming **hypotheses** (ideas scientists explore), conducting experiments, and analyzing the results.

To test the effects of a new food product, scientists divide test animals into at least two groups. One group does not receive the new food. This is the **control** group, the group that is subject to normal conditions.

Other groups of test animals are fed different amounts of the new food. The new food is the **variable**, the factor that differs among the test groups. All other factors are kept the same among all the groups.

If the animals in all the groups remain healthy, then the experiment provides evidence that the new food is safe. But if illness in the animals increases with the new food in their diet, then this may be evidence that the food is harmful.

LAWS AND POLICIES

People have been experimenting on animals since ancient times. In ancient Rome, a physician named Galen cut open farm animals and studied their parts. This helped him form useful ideas about the human body. (Not all of his ideas proved correct.)

Today, in many countries, Galen's treatment of animals would be carefully regulated. Many laws and policies protect **animal welfare**. Scientists also work together to promote animal-friendly practices.

Here is a summary of the guidelines that apply to laboratories in the United States. Other countries have similar guidelines. However, scientists may interpret them in different ways.

Useful purposes
Scientists should conduct experiments on animals for useful purposes only. A useful purpose could be improved human health, improved animal health, or the gain of scientific knowledge.

Limited numbers
Scientists should choose the proper type and number of animals for an experiment.

No pain
Animals should suffer as little pain or discomfort as possible. A test animal should receive medication to ease any pain or discomfort.

Experts only
Trained, professional scientists should conduct or supervise all experiments on live animals.

Must end
An experiment on live animals should be designed with a clear end point. It should not end only when a desired result is reached.

LIFE OR DEATH?

Policies for laboratory animals protect them from unnecessary pain and suffering. They also prevent many forms of cruelty to animals. However many animals used in research are killed once the experiment is completed.

Sometimes the tests will kill or weaken the animals. Many of the animals are killed when the experiment ends because the scientists need to examine inside their bodies to see what effect a drug has had on them. Policies make sure that the animals are well taken care of while they are alive.

Lab animals, like this guinea pig, are likely to be killed once an experiment is over. But they are protected by guidelines and policies which make sure they are kept in very good conditions. Some are even adopted as pets when their time in the lab is over.

ANIMALS IN THE LAB

Not everyone agrees that animal testing is worthwhile. <u>Critics argue that animal testing is too expensive and not useful</u>. Many critics also cite ethical issues. **Ethics** is the study of right and wrong.

HIGH COST

All animals need food, water, and space to live in. An animal-testing laboratory must spend money on food and cages, and find room to store the animals. Staff must be paid to maintain the animals, sometimes 24 hours a day and on weekends.

As a general rule, the cost of keeping an animal increases with the animal's size. The larger the animal, the more food and care it needs. Large animals also tend to have babies less frequently and in small numbers. This is one reason why mice and rabbits are common test animals, while moose and giraffes are not. It's easy to breed lots of mice!

HOW EFFECTIVE IS ANIMAL TESTING?

Mice and other test animals resemble humans in many ways. But they clearly are not identical to humans. In a laboratory, test animals are kept in cages. They may be subject to stress not found in their natural environment. Critics argue that this stress changes their response to foods and drugs.

How effective is animal testing? Hidden data would help answer this question. During the past 50 years, many drugs, food additives, and **cosmetics** have been tested on animals. But companies often keep private the results of these tests. They don't want their competitors to benefit from the research.

Test monkeys

Monkeys are useful test animals because they are from the same animal group that includes humans. A study of monkeys led to a better understanding of human blood. And in the 1960s, monkeys were trained as astronauts.

Today, monkeys are not as common in laboratories as before. One reason is the high cost of keeping them. Another reason is that the public has objected to the use of monkeys as test subjects.

COSMETICS

Cosmetics are products that help people stay healthy or be attractive. They include soap, shampoo, lotions, and makeup.

In the years after World War II, cosmetics became increasingly popular. But some consumers reported that certain cosmetics hurt their eyes or skin, or caused other unwanted effects. In response, cosmetic companies began testing new products on animals.

In one common test, eye makeup was applied repeatedly to the eyes of rabbits. The rabbits were given much more makeup than people would ever use, and they were eventually blinded. Other tests measured the lethal (deadly) dosage of a cosmetic. Critics argued that the tests were cruel, painful, and unnecessary.

Today, most cosmetics are not tested on animals.

Issues of animal welfare attract attention all over the world. This protest took place in Malaysia.

TESTING TODAY

Over the years, people have become more aware of animal testing in the cosmetics industry. Today, the practice is banned in many countries in Europe and it is declining elsewhere. The U.S. Food and Drug Administration does not require cosmetics to be tested on animals.

Cosmetics companies are now using other methods to ensure the safety of their products. Many tests are performed on samples of animal parts instead of the whole animal. Other tests involve studying the cosmetics themselves. Scientists are also investigating new kinds of tests.

NO MORE TESTING!

The European Union (group of European countries that pass laws together) has passed a law to ban animal testing for cosmetics. But complete enforcement of the law has been delayed. The reason is that replacement tests have not been developed yet.

The European Cosmetics Association, or Colipa, represents over 2,000 cosmetics companies from many nations. Here is a statement about animal testing made in 2009 by Bertil Heerink, the director of Colipa:

"Our industry's commitment to replacing animal testing stretches back long before bans were put in place. We play a leading role in the development of new alternative methods and will continue to work together with other key partners, in order to move towards the goal of replacing animal testing completely."

13

REPLACING THE DOG LAB

For many years, Michigan State University required veterinary students to practice surgery on live dogs. The dogs were raised specifically for use in laboratories. After the operations, the dogs were **euthanized**, or killed, with as little pain as possible.

Then in 2010, at the urging of many **animal rights** groups, the school ended this requirement. To replace their work in the dog lab, veterinary students now study computer models or programs and practice on animal **cadavers**. A cadaver is a dead body.

The decision was controversial among students and the public. Read some of the comments on the issue on the next page.

FOR DOG LABS

- "A great surgeon is not made from a computer program. It takes a lot of practice on live animals."

- "My first surgery was the most frightening event of my life. I can't imagine how scared I would have felt if I was operating on someone's pet."

AGAINST DOG LABS

- "A vet should respect the life of all animals, not just the ones owned by the right people."

- "What does it say for us and our profession that we kill animals in order to teach students how to heal them? Seems a bit hypocritical to me."

ANIMALS FOR EDUCATION

In many laboratories, animals are used to train science students, doctors, or **veterinarians**. Biology students often dissect (pick apart and study) the body of a dead animal, such as a frog. Medical students sometimes use dogs to practice a surgical operation.

While animals are still used for education and training, the practice is becoming less common. At many schools, computer simulations have replaced or partially replaced real animal subjects. The software is less expensive than experimenting on real animals. The software is also less messy.

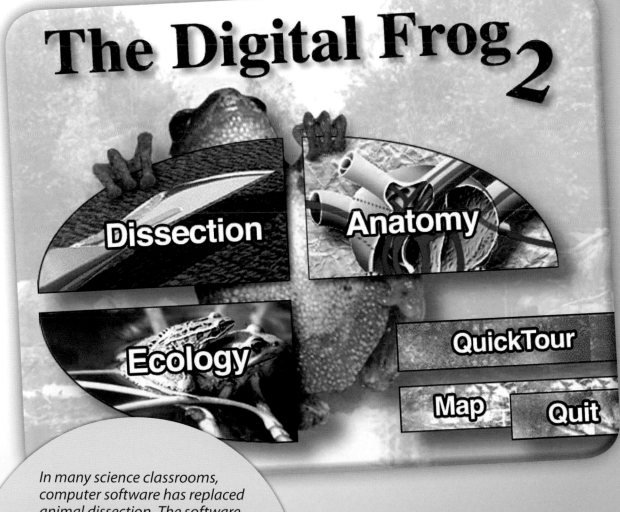

The Digital Frog 2

Dissection

Anatomy

Ecology

QuickTour

Map

Quit

In many science classrooms, computer software has replaced animal dissection. The software is "frog friendly", but is it the best choice for biology students? What do you think?

ETHICAL QUESTIONS

Ethics is the study of right and wrong. Scientists face a wide variety of ethical questions in their dealings with animals. Like other ethical questions, the ethical questions involving **animal welfare** may not have easy answers. Here are some ethical questions. As you read them, consider how you would answer them. How certain are you that your answers and ideas are the right ones?

DOES SPECIES MATTER?

Scientists conduct laboratory experiments on a wide variety of animal **species**, including monkeys, dogs, cats, and mice. Does the species of the animal affect whether an experiment is right or wrong? Does the intelligence or awareness of the animal make a difference?

Remember that the animal kingdom also includes insects, worms, and other **invertebrates** (animals without backbones). Few people object to laboratory experiments on insects.

DOES THE GOAL MATTER?

Laboratory animals may be treated with unusual drugs or chemicals, or fed harmful foods. They may be subjected to surgical operations. Are these practices acceptable only for some goals, such as curing diseases? Can animal welfare be compromised for a good cause?

Laboratory animals have no knowledge of a scientist's purpose, nor could they evaluate it. Scientists and society must decide whether an experiment's goal is worthy of animal testing.

DOES AN ANIMAL'S HISTORY MATTER?

Many breeders raise animals specifically for animal testing, and they supply the animals for most experiments. In certain cases, some laboratories accept unwanted dogs and cats from pounds and shelters.

Is raising animals specifically for testing an ethical practice? Many stray dogs and cats are **euthanized** if no one claims them. Are these animals better candidates for animal testing?

NEW QUESTIONS

In the past 200 years, the human population has increased drastically – from about one billion people in 1800 to almost seven billion people today. Human technology has improved greatly, too.

Because society has changed and become more complex, our relationship with animals has also become more complex. As a result, scientists and the public face many new ethical questions that involve animals. Science alone cannot answer all of these questions. While scientists bring a useful viewpoint to ethical questions, they apply their own opinions and values to the answers they suggest.

GENETIC TECHNOLOGY

Genes are made of **DNA**. DNA codes for all the traits of a living thing. A trait is a feature of a living thing, such as body shape, size, and colour. In recent years, scientists have invented many new technologies for changing or manipulating genes. Some of these technologies are very controversial.

For example, scientists have made **clones** (exact genetic duplicates) of animals. They have produced **genetically modified (GM)** salmon that grow twice as fast as other salmon. Genetically modified animals have had their genes changed by scientists. Other similar animals may soon be produced.

Are practices like these ethically acceptable? Not everyone agrees that they are. Even so, genetic technology continues to develop and become more common.

Ghandi's words

Mahatma Gandhi (1869-1948) was a political and spiritual leader of India. He is remembered for arguing against violence, even in the face of oppression. Here are his thoughts about humans and animals:

"The greatness of a nation and its moral progress can be judged by the way its animals are treated."

UNFAIR ADVANTAGES?

Technology gives humans the advantage in nearly all their dealings with animals. For example, fishing boats can find fish with special devices that bounce sounds through the water. Deer and moose are no match for hunters with powerful, accurate rifles.

Does technology give humans an unfair advantage? The answer depends on what people think is fair in the relationship between humans and animals.

For hundreds of years, people caught fish with simple boats and nets. The top photo shows Native Alaskans and their fish catch in 1903. Today, most fishermen use more advanced technology.

SCIENCE, FARMS, AND RANCHES

All over the world, scientists work with farmers and ranchers to help them raise animals. They work for governments, universities, and private companies. Scientists help farmers and ranchers breed animals, provide animals the best diet, and produce meat and other foods of high quality. Many scientists also promote the humane treatment of farm and ranch animals.

ANIMAL BREEDING

People developed the many breeds of cattle, pigs, chickens, and other farm animals through a process called **selective breeding**. In this process, the breeder chooses a mating pair who have desired characteristics, such as a stocky body for beef cattle or high milk production for dairy cattle. After many generations, the desired characteristics become enhanced in the offspring.

Today, scientists work with farmers and ranchers to develop the most useful breeds. They also work to keep the breeds healthy.

Temple Grandin

For many years, Dr. Temple Grandin argued that the welfare of livestock affects the quality of their meat. Eventually, the ranching industry began to listen. Today, her ideas on minimizing the stress and suffering of livestock are applied to stockades and feedlots.

In 2010, *Time* magazine listed Dr. Grandin as one of the 100 most influential people in the world.

Most dairy farms rely on automatic milking machines and other technology to manage cattle.

CATTLE RANCHING

In the western United States, herds of beef cattle once grazed on the open prairie. Now many ranchers keep beef cattle in large pens, called stockades, where food is brought to the cattle. This practice helps cattle grow larger and faster. It also helps ranchers control costs and sell meat at a high price.

Scientists helped ranchers develop the technique for modern cattle raising. They are also voicing concerns about these practices. One concern is that cattle are prone to infections in the crowded pens. The cattle are given **antibiotics**, which are drugs that kill **bacteria**. Bacteria are tiny living things that can cause disease. But bacteria will develop resistance to any widely used antibiotic over time.

THE OLDER WAY OF RAISING ANIMALS

For most of human history, farmers raised animals on pastures and other open lands. Cows and sheep grazed on grass, chickens scratched for seeds and scraps, and pigs dug for roots. Many scientists, farmers, and consumers are now promoting this older way of raising animals. They argue that the animals are healthier and happier. They also claim that the meat, milk, and eggs are tastier and better for human health.

Hundreds of years ago, scenes like this one were common all over the world. Today, many cattle and sheep are fed in stockades and feedlots.

Backyard farms

Rural families have always kept goats, chickens, and other farm animals. Now many cities and suburbs allow people to raise farm animals in their backyards. With fencing and a shed, people can turn their backyard into a goat pen or chicken coop. Hey, who wants fresh eggs for breakfast?

HEALTHY ANIMALS

Why does the quality of meat depend on the way a cow or chicken is raised? One way to answer this question is to study how animals live in the wild. Animals survive in the wild only when they can meet their needs for food, water, air, and shelter.

An **adaptation** is a special body part or behaviour that helps an animal survive. The long beak of a pelican is an adaptation for catching fish. The sharp claws and teeth of a lion are adaptations for tearing meat.

Farm animals also have adaptations. Cows have flat teeth, a four-part stomach, and other adaptations for grazing. Chickens peck and scratch, which are behavioural adaptations for finding food.

On farms where animals roam fields, they live by using their body adaptations and practising their adapted behaviours. They cannot live like this in stockades or other tightly controlled environments.

ANIMALS IN THE WILD

Many wild animals may never interact with humans. Yet human actions still affect their lives and welfare. As the human population keeps increasing, the land available for wildlife has been decreasing. Wild animals also suffer from human activities such as overhunting, pollution, and spreading harmful plants and animals to new places.

This researcher is placing a radio collar on a wild wolf. He will use the collar to track the wolf and learn more about how to help wolves in the wild.

Endangered species

An endangered species is a species that has a low population and might soon go extinct. Scientists have identified over a thousand endangered species worldwide. Species are endangered in every country of the world, and in every U.S. state.

As forests are cut down, the habitat for forest animals becomes smaller and smaller.

HABITAT DESTRUCTION

A **habitat** is the home of a plant or animal. In places around the world, the natural habitats of many animals are being taken over for human use. For example, during the past 20 years, Brazil lost over 320,000 square miles (828,800 square kilometres) of rain forest. This is an area four times the size of England!

Scientists are concerned that as habitats are destroyed, plant and animal species are being lost, too. An extinct species no longer has any members alive. Some rain forest species may go extinct without scientists ever identifying them.

STOPPING THE DESTRUCTION

Many scientists have joined concerned people and business leaders to fight habitat destruction and to protect wildlife. They often work through organizations such as the World Wildlife Fund, the Sierra Club, and the Rainforest Action Network. These organizations and many others have the same goal, which is to protect wilderness regions and wildlife while there is still time.

THREATS FROM INVADERS

Another threat to wild animals comes from **invasive species**. <u>An invasive species is a species that enters a new environment and grows there rapidly.</u> As the invaders spread and grow, they harm native plants and wildlife.

One example of an invasive animal is the cane toad. The cane toad causes few problems in its native region, which is Central and South America. But in the 1930s, cane toads were taken to Australia to help fight farm pests. Unfortunately, the results were terrible. Today, the Australian population of cane toads is over 200 million!

Cane toads eat almost any food they can find. This leaves less food for native frogs and toads. But cane toads are also harming larger animals because they are poisonous. The **predators** of South America have learned to avoid cane toads. But in Australia, the predators are snapping up cane toads – and getting sick or dying as a result.

When invaders like this cane toad arrive, they can harm the welfare of native species.

HELP FROM SCIENTISTS

Today, scientists recognize the damage that invasive species can cause. Scientists help governments keep invaders away from sensitive environments. They also look for ways to control invaders after they have arrived.

Jane Goodall

As a young girl, Jane Goodall was fond of a stuffed toy chimp named Jubilee. She still has the toy, which she says nurtured her lifelong interest in chimpanzees.

For months at a time, Goodall lived with groups of chimps in the forests of Tanzania, in Africa. She observed them carefully and respectfully, eventually gaining their trust. Among her observations were that chimps made and used tools and used language to communicate. She concluded that chimps were more like humans than anyone had imagined.

Today, Goodall helps run the Jane Goodall Institute. The mission of the institute is to protect the habitat and promote the welfare of chimps, apes, and other wildlife.

This photo shows Dr. Jane Goodall and an orangutan.

In the 1950s, most zoos kept animals in cages made of wires, glass, or wood. The cages did not look like the animals' natural habitats.

ZOOS AND AQUARIUMS

The oldest existing zoo is in Vienna, Austria. It opened to the public in 1765. Zoos soon became popular in cities across Europe, and then later in North America and elsewhere.

Zoos and aquariums (buildings with tanks full of water animals) have always let city dwellers observe and interact with wild animals from around the world. Today, however, these institutions have broader missions. Zoos and aquariums help protect wildlife, train scientists, and educate the public about animal **conservation**. Conservation is keeping a resource so that future generations can use it.

CAPTIVE BREEDING PROGRAMS

As you have read, many animal species are facing extinction in the wild. To save them, zoos participate in captive breeding programs. Scientists select a mating pair, then let them raise their young in as natural conditions as possible. When feasible, the young are reintroduced to their native homes.

Captive breeding programmes have helped rescue many species, such as black-footed ferrets and California condors. But other species have proved difficult for scientists to breed. Some scientists argue that money should be spent on protecting natural habitats of animals, not on captive breeding.

LEARNING AT THE ZOO

Zoos employ **veterinarians**, animal nutritionists, and other scientists who study animals. These scientists both care for the animals and learn from them. Many **marine biologists** study and train at aquariums.

The next time you visit a zoo, read or listen to facts about the animals on display. You can also take classes or attend lectures there, or learn how to promote wildlife conservation in your region.

Today, zoos try to recreate an animal's habitat in the wild.

LIVES OF PETS

If you own a pet, then you know that the pet's welfare is your responsibility. Dogs, cats, and other pets depend on their owners to meet all of their needs, including food, water, shelter, and health care. **Veterinarians** help keep pets healthy, and other scientists help to develop nutritious pet food and other pet products. But ultimately, pet owners must choose what they think is best for their animals.

Owning a pet brings many responsibilities – and many rewards.

SPAYING AND NEUTERING

Homeless and unwanted dogs and cats are a problem in cities all over the world. When they are caught, they may be kept in animal shelters for a week or longer, but not indefinitely. Many are **euthanized**.

To help manage this problem, **animal welfare** organizations recommend that pet dogs and cats be spayed or neutered. The operation does not harm the animal's welfare and it prevents unwanted puppies and kittens.

DECLAWING

Surgically removing a cat's claws is illegal in Europe but allowed in the United States. Opponents argue that declawing is cruel and painful. Yet many cat owners request it to stop cats from ruining furniture and fabrics.

Should declawing be banned because it is cruel to cats? If it was banned, would the number of homeless or abandoned cats increase? What do you think is the right choice?

Saying goodbye

When a pet becomes old or sick, owners may face some tough decisions. A veterinarian might offer or recommend treatments, but cannot guarantee the outcome. And some treatments, especially surgeries, are very expensive. Often the alternative is euthanasia to prevent unnecessary suffering.

Here is a quote from one pet owner:

"When you accept a pet dog or cat into your home, you accept the job of caring for it. This includes saying goodbye when the time comes."

BREEDING DOGS

People have been breeding dogs for thousands of years. Dog breeds today include very large dogs, such as mastiffs and Great Danes; very small ones, such as Chihuahuas; and dogs of many shapes and sizes in between.

Dogs are bred much like farm animals. The breeder chooses parents with desirable traits, such as large size, fast speed, even personality, or an attractive coat. Then the puppies are evaluated for their traits.

Professional breeders follow strict rules for ensuring the dogs' welfare. Yet they also face some ethical questions. For example, dalmatians are popular for their spotted coats, but they are also prone to deafness. Is it acceptable to breed an animal for its appearance but not for health?

Sheepdogs are bred for their large size, long coats, and herding abilities.

Preventing cruelty to animals

In England, the Royal Society for the Prevention of Cruelty to Animals (RSPCA) was founded in 1824. An American society (ASPCA) was founded a number of years later. These organizations promote animal welfare in many ways, including lobbying for new laws and helping police enforce existing laws. Many scientists are active in both organizations.

A puppy mill is a breeding facility that keeps dogs in terrible, inhumane conditions. Both the RSPCA and ASPCA have helped governments find and close down puppy mills.

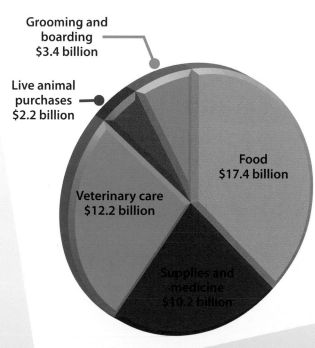

Collars, treats, toys, and grooming equipment are just some of the purchases people make for their pets.

MONEY FOR PETS

Pet owners everywhere spend a huge amount of money on food, health care, and other products and services for their pets. In 2009, $45 billion was spent on pets in the United States alone. And this does not include the money spent on animal shelters and other community services.

Some scientists wish that people would spend even part of this money to help wildlife. Dogs and cats are in no danger of becoming **extinct**. Would money spent on operations for ageing pets be better spent on endangered animals? What is your opinion?

Money spent on pets in the United States (2009)

Grooming and boarding
$3.4 billion

Live animal purchases
$2.2 billion

Food
$17.4 billion

Veterinary care
$12.2 billion

Supplies and medicine
$10.2 billion

33

OCEAN ANIMALS

Oceans cover three-fourths of Earth's surface. They are home to a tremendous variety of animals, from fish the size of your index finger to the blue whale, which is larger than a school bus. Yet many ocean animals are at risk. As scientists are concluding, ocean animals are in danger from pollution and **habitat** destruction. The struggles of ocean animals are much like those of wildlife on land.

EUGENIE CLARK: THE SHARK LADY

At age nine, Eugenie Clark was fascinated by the sharks she observed at an aquarium. Eventually she took a job at that aquarium. Today she is an expert on fish of all kinds, and sharks especially. She was one of the first scientists to study fish by putting on scuba gear and swimming with them.

In 1955, Clark founded a laboratory that today is the Mote Marine Laboratory in Sarasota, Florida. The laboratory's mission is to study oceans and ocean animals, help protect and conserve the ocean environment, and educate the public.

In 2010, a huge amount of oil spilled spread across the Gulf of Mexico, killing most of the marine life it touched. These brown pelicans were rescued by an organization that protects wildlife.

CORAL REEFS

Coral may look like an underwater plant that lives on rock. But corals are animals. They make a type of hard material that builds up on the ocean floor. This material makes up a coral reef.

A coral reef is home to a large and diverse community of corals, fish, and other marine animals. It may be the most diverse community on Earth. Yet coral reefs are in trouble worldwide. Corals are very sensitive to changes in the temperature and the pH (acidity) of the water. Such changes are occurring now, perhaps as a result of **global climate change** (see pages 38–39).

Scientists are concerned that if coral reefs die, the oceans will lose many types of fish and other animals. They are urging nations to pass laws to protect reefs.

PROTECTING THE OCEANS

Ocean scientists have proposed many laws and policies to help protect ocean animals. They also work with shipping companies, fishermen, oil companies, and other businesses and industries that affect ocean life.

Here are some of their accomplishments, as well as some challenges they still are trying to meet.

Marine reserves

Fishermen used to catch boatloads of many fish **species**, including halibut, Atlantic cod, and swordfish. But today the populations of these fish are very low. The cause is overfishing, which is the catching of more fish than the population can quickly replace.

To combat overfishing, scientists have urged nations to establish **marine reserves**. These are regions of the water where fishing is banned. They hope that fish species can recover in the reserves. Today, most nations have established marine reserves. Reserves include the Great Barrier Reef of Australia and the Florida Keys National Marine Sanctuary.

No whaling

Many species of whales were hunted almost to extinction. Scientists convinced many nations, including the United States, to ban whaling and the hunting of dolphins. But whaling is still allowed in some countries.

Stopping pollution

Many human activities can pollute ocean waters, either by accident or through carelessness. Perhaps the worst pollution has come from oil spills. In 2010, an explosion caused an oil pipe in the Gulf of Mexico to burst apart. Oil flowed into the water for three months, killing wildlife across hundreds of square miles. The spill will take years to clean up completely.

The work of scientists helps to clean up oil spills and prevent them from happening. Some scientists have called for a ban on oil drilling in the ocean. But people need oil, and ocean drilling seems likely to continue.

Laws now protect the hunting of whales and dolphins. Nevertheless, many dolphins are caught in tuna nets. Tuna and dolphins often swim together.

To prevent spills, tankers must now hold oil inside an inner hull that is separated from the outer hull.

Global climate change

What is the biggest threat to the welfare of wildlife? According to many scientists, the biggest threat is **global climate change** (also called global warming). Scientists warn that human actions are causing gradual changes to Earth's climate. Because animals depend on the climate, their welfare will suffer.

CLIMATE AND ANIMALS

Scientists agree that Earth's temperatures have gradually been warming. Most scientists identify the cause of the warming to be humans' use of **fossil fuels**, such as coal and oil. The burning of these fuels adds carbon dioxide to the **atmosphere**. Carbon dioxide helps trap heat on Earth's surface.

Why do animals depend on the climate? Remember that animals have **adaptations** that help them survive in their environments. But adaptations may take thousands, even millions of years to develop. Many animals may not adapt to climate change in time.

Like wildlife everywhere, the animals of the African savanna are adapted to a certain type of environment that is controlled by climate.

Climate change has been especially severe in polar regions.

In Antarctica, for example, populations of many penguin **species** are dropping rapidly. The penguins are struggling to find their way along the melting coastline!

FIGHTING CLIMATE CHANGE

Many scientists have joined the fight against climate change. They are working together to convince governments, industries, and the public that the problem is real and needs to be addressed.

If scientists' predictions are correct, climate change will get worse before it gets better. A solution will come only when people switch away from fossil fuels and stop increasing the carbon dioxide levels in the atmosphere.

"So what if some don't believe in global warming? They're wrong.... Time to stop dithering and get serious about policies that could make a difference."

—Martin Hoffert, physics professor, New York University

"The scientific evidence is clear: global climate change caused by human activities is occurring now, and it is a growing threat to society."

—Statement from the American Association for the Advancement of Science (AAAS)

CAREERS in animal science

If you enjoy science and care about animals, you can combine both interests with a career in animal science. Many kinds of scientists study animals and promote **animal welfare**. Here are just a few of the careers to choose from.

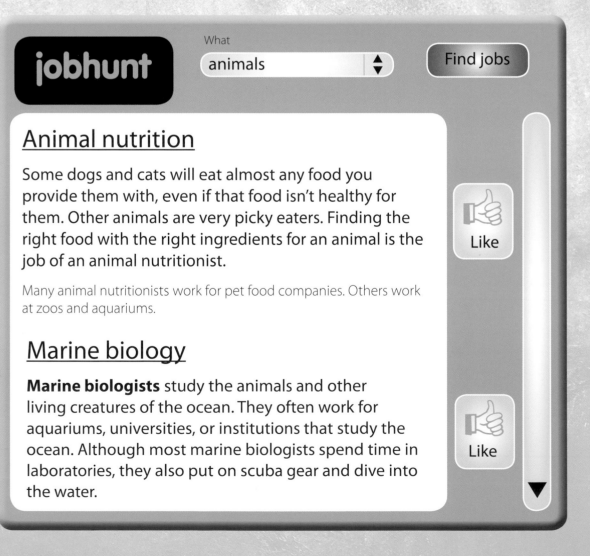

jobhunt

What

animals

Find jobs

Animal nutrition

Some dogs and cats will eat almost any food you provide them with, even if that food isn't healthy for them. Other animals are very picky eaters. Finding the right food with the right ingredients for an animal is the job of an animal nutritionist.

Many animal nutritionists work for pet food companies. Others work at zoos and aquariums.

Like

Marine biology

Marine biologists study the animals and other living creatures of the ocean. They often work for aquariums, universities, or institutions that study the ocean. Although most marine biologists spend time in laboratories, they also put on scuba gear and dive into the water.

Like

Veterinary medicine

Many **veterinarians** (or vets, for short) treat people's dogs and cats. Others treat farm animals, especially large animals such as cows, sheep, and pigs. Vets also work for zoos, aquariums, science laboratories, and any institution where animals are kept.

Becoming a vet requires four years of college, then at least four years of training in a school of veterinary medicine. These schools are very competitive. They choose candidates who demonstrate strong science skills and an interest in helping animals and people.

Other careers in veterinary medicine include veterinary nurse and veterinary technologist.

Like

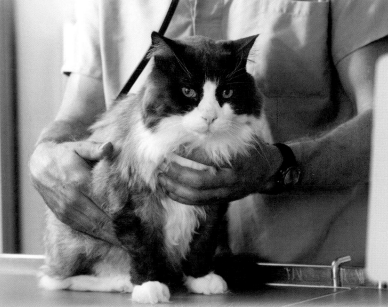

"By loving and understanding animals, perhaps we humans shall come to understand each other."

—*Dr. Louis J. Camuti, veterinarian*

SUMMARY

Animal welfare is the well-being and health of animals. Either directly or indirectly, human actions affect the welfare of all animals on Earth. These animals include wildlife, farm animals, pet dogs and cats, and animals used for experimentation in laboratories.

Is it ethical to conduct experiments on animals, especially when the animal dies as a result of the experiment? Does the purpose of the research make a difference in the **ethics**, or is the intelligence of the animal **species** important? People struggle to answer these questions and others like them. They do not have easy answers.

Many scientists study animals and help humans interact with animals. Some scientists work with cattle and other farm animals, and some study wild animals on land or in the ocean. **Veterinarians** and other scientists help people take care of pets. All kinds of scientists work hard to educate the public about animals and help governments enact wise laws and policies.

QUESTIONS TO DISCUSS

Do you support these laws and policies for handling laboratory animals? Do you think they are sufficient for protecting animal welfare?	**Pages 8-9**
Do you have strong opinions about these ethical issues? Or would you struggle to resolve them?	**Pages 16-17**
Do you ever think about the animals that are the source of the meat, eggs, and other foods that you eat? Are you concerned about how they were raised?	**Pages 22-23**
Have you or your family ever made a difficult decision about the life of a pet? How did you reach this decision?	**Pages 30-31**
Would you be interested in a science career that involves animals?	**Pages 40-41**

Glossary

adaptation body structure or inborn behavior that helps an organism survive in its environment

anatomy body structure of an animal or human

animal rights idea that animals have moral rights, as humans do

animal welfare well-being of animals

antibiotic drug that helps the body kill bacteria

atmosphere layer of gases that surrounds Earth and other planets

bacteria single-celled microorganism

cadaver dead body of an animal

clone exact genetic duplicate

conservation wise use of a resource so that it is available in the future

control in an experiment, a test group that is treated under normal conditions

cosmetic product applied to the body to promote beauty

DNA deoxyribonucleic acid, the molecule that codes for traits in all organisms

endangered species type of living thing that has a very low population and is at risk of extinction

ethics study of right and wrong

euthanized killed for merciful reasons

extinct species that has died out completely

fossil fuels fuels such as coal and petroleum (oil) that were formed underground from the remains of plants and animals

gene part of the genetic information of a living thing. Most genes tell cells how to make a particular protein.

genetically modified (GM) having genes that have been artificially altered

global climate change gradual rise in the average temperature of Earth's surface, also called global warming

habitat environment in which a plant or animal lives

hypothesis idea that scientists try to prove through experiments

invasive species species that arrives in a new environment and thrives there, harming native species

invertebrate animal without a backbone

marine biologist scientist who studies the living things of the ocean

marine reserve region of the ocean where animals are protected from fishing and other human activities

parasite animal or organism that lives in or on another animal (its host) and gets some of its food from that animal

predator animal that hunts, kills, and eats other animals

puppy mill facility where dogs are bred without regard to their welfare

scientific method system of observation, testing, and reasoning that scientists use to develop explanations of nature

selective breeding choosing of mating pairs to produce desired traits in offspring

species type of living thing

variable factor that differs among the test groups of an experiment

veterinarian person who treats sick or injured animals

Find out more

Books

Animal Rights and Testing (Ethical Debates) by Patience Coster (Wayland, 2011)

Animal Rights (Introducing Issues With Opposing Viewpoints) by Lauri S. Friedman (Greenhaven Press, 2010)

Animal Welfare (What's That Got to do With Me?) by Antony Lishak (Franklin Watts, 2009)

Unloved and Endangered Animals: What You Can Do (Green Issues in Focus) by Cindy Watson (Enslow Publishers, 2010)

Zoos and Animal Welfare (Issues that Concern You) by Christine Van Tuyl (Greenhaven Press, 2007)

Websites

http://animaldiversity.ummz.umich.edu/site/index.html
Here is a huge online encyclopedia of animals, searchable by the name of species or class.

www.awionline.org/
Read about the latest news and initiatives for animal welfare around the world.

www.dosomething.org/
Learn how you can make a difference in animal welfare and other important issues.

www.worldwildlife.org
Read about the issues affecting wildlife all over the world, and ways that you can help wildlife.

Topics to research

Animals and the science classroom

Are animals dissected in science classrooms in your school? Find out why or why not. Interview science teachers, science students, and other school officials to learn their opinions about the use of animals in science education.

Animal shelters

Research an animal shelter that serves your community. Who sponsors the shelter? How are animals treated there? Are dogs and cats from the shelter available for adoption?

Zoos and aquariums

Research the treatment of animals at a zoo or aquarium that serves your community.

Wildlife

What issues face the wild animals that live in your state or region? Are any of these animals endangered? If so, are steps being taken to protect them? Find out and report your findings.

Index

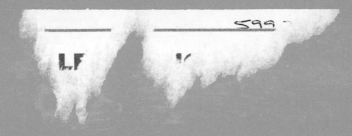

599

LF

LIVING IN THE WILD: BIG CATS

Charlotte Guillain

Raintree is an imprint of Capstone Global Library Limited, a company incorporated in England and Wales having its registered office at 7 Pilgrim Street, London, EC4V 6LB – Registered company number: 6695582

www.raintreepublishers.co.uk
myorders@raintreepublishers.co.uk

Edited by Clare Lewis and Adrian Vigliano
Designed by Tim Bond
Original illustrations © HL Studios
Picture research by Tracy Cummins
Originated by Capstone Global Library Ltd
Printed and bound in China

ISBN 978 1 406 27343 4
17 16 15 14 13
10 9 8 7 6 5 4 3 2 1

A full catalogue record for this book is available from the British Library.

Acknowledgments

The author and publisher are grateful to the following for permission to reproduce copyright material:
AP Photo p. 25 (Milwaukee County Zoo); Getty Images pp. 11 (Tom Brakefield), 16 (Suzi Eszterhas), 17 (Carol Farneti-Foster), 20 (SA Team/ Foto Natura), 22 (Brian Mckay Photography), 33 (Panoramic Images), 35, 45 (Mint Images - Frans Lanting), 37 (José Enrique Molina), 43 (Gerry Ellis); National Geographic Stock pp. 23, 31 (SA TEAM/ FOTO NATURA/ MINDEN PIC), 29 (FRANS LANTING), 39 (STEVE WINTER); Nature Picture Library p. 19 (Luiz Claudio Marigo); Newscom p. 41 (EPA/Francisco Guasco); Shutterstock pp. 6 (Matt Gibson), 7 (Ewan Chesser), 9 (Hedrus), 12, 15 (Pal Teravagimov), 18 (TOMO); Superstock pp. 5 (Minden Pictures), 13 (NHPA), 24, 27 (Gerard Lacz / age footstock), 34 (age footstock).

Cover photograph of a jaguar reproduced with permission of Getty Images (Mint Images - Frans Lanting).

We would like to thank Michael Bright for his invaluable help in the preparation of this book.

Every effort has been made to contact copyright holders of any material reproduced in this book. Any omissions will be rectified in subsequent printings if notice is given to the publisher.

Disclaimer

Contents

Some words are shown in bold, **like this**. You can find out what they mean by looking in the glossary.

What are big cats?

A shadow moves through the trees of a tropical forest. It moves silently towards an unsuspecting deer, getting closer and closer. Suddenly the dark shape leaps out and seizes the deer in a deadly bite. This powerful killer is a jaguar.

Jaguars are mammals that are included in a group called big cats. The term 'big cat' has different meanings, but generally refers to the larger wild cats, such as jaguars, lions, tigers, leopards, pumas, cheetahs, snow leopards, and clouded leopards. Sometimes the term big cat is used more specifically to include the larger cats that can roar. These are jaguars, lions, tigers, and leopards only.

As well as being able to roar, this smaller group of big cats shares the following features:

- They are all above a certain size.
- They are all carnivores.
- They are all **apex predators**. This means no other animal hunts them for food.

BIG CAT NAME

The word 'jaguar' comes from an American Indian word, *yaguará*. This is thought to mean 'large beast of **prey**' or possibly 'he who kills with one leap'.

Jaguars spend a lot of time around or in water.

Big cats live in different parts of the world in a range of **habitats**. These include the grasslands of Africa, the forests of North America, the mountains of Southeast Asia, and the swamplands of South America. Some, such as tigers and jaguars, are good swimmers. Some, such as pumas and leopards, live alone, while lions live in large groups called prides. All big cats have coloured or patterned coats that help to conceal them as they hunt prey.

5

What are jaguars?

The jaguar is one of the largest, most powerful big cats and is the biggest cat in North and South America. A jaguar has a similar coat to a leopard, with golden-brownish fur patterned with dark spots, called **rosettes**. Sometimes the spots on a jaguar's back blend together to look like a stripe. This fearsome hunter has a strong, sturdy, muscular body, with a large head and powerful jaws. Jaguars can vary in size according to where they live, but the males are always much larger than the females. A male jaguar can weigh as much as 160 kilograms (350 pounds), while the heaviest females weigh about 85 kilograms (187 pounds).

Black panthers

Some jaguars and leopards have completely black fur and are often called black panthers. Animals that have black fur rather than the typical colouring for their **species** are described as **melanistic**. A change in their **genes** has made this happen. Scientists think the black fur helps to **camouflage** the jaguar in darker places and so it has become a useful **adaptation** for survival.

A female jaguar can have some cubs with patterned coats and some with black fur in the same **litter**.

SPECIAL SPOTS

In the same way that every human has a unique set of fingerprints, the rosettes on a jaguar's coat are in a different pattern for every individual. This helps scientists studying jaguars to identify different cats and monitor population numbers. A jaguar's rosettes are different from a leopard's as they have a dot or dots in the middle, while a leopard's do not.

How are jaguars classified?

All living things are put into groups, or **classified**, by scientists. This helps to identify every living thing accurately and to explain how and why they live where they do. Classification means grouping living things according to the features that they share.

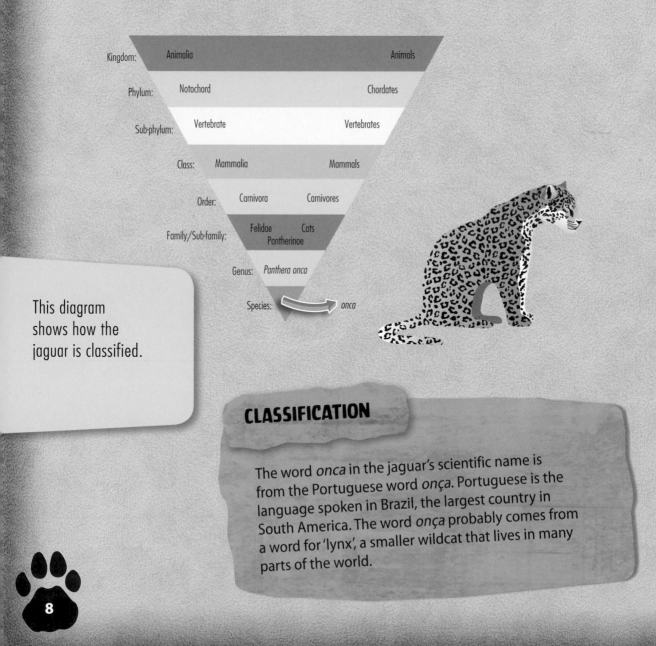

Kingdom:	Animalia	Animals
Phylum:	Notochord	Chordates
Sub-phylum:	Vertebrate	Vertebrates
Class:	Mammalia	Mammals
Order:	Carnivora	Carnivores
Family/Sub-family:	Felidae Cats Pantherinae	
Genus:	*Panthera onca*	
Species:		*onca*

This diagram shows how the jaguar is classified.

CLASSIFICATION

The word *onca* in the jaguar's scientific name is from the Portuguese word *onça*. Portuguese is the language spoken in Brazil, the largest country in South America. The word *onça* probably comes from a word for 'lynx', a smaller wildcat that lives in many parts of the world.

Classification groups

Classification triangles are used to show how each living thing is classified. Towards the bottom of the triangle each group contains fewer and fewer members. For example, there are fewer animals in the order Carnivora (carnivores) than there are in the class Mammalia (mammals), and so on.

Jaguars are in the family Felidae, which includes all cats, large and small, wild and domesticated.

Special cats

Living things are given a scientific name, such as *Panthera onca*, so they have a single name rather than many different names in different languages. Sometimes living things are grouped into subspecies within a species because of small differences between them. There are no subspecies of jaguar but their size varies in different regions.

Leopards look similar to jaguars but have longer bodies and are slimmer and lighter.

Where do jaguars live?

All wild animals live in a habitat. This is the place where an animal can find everything it needs to live, such as food, water, and shelter. Jaguars live in a range of habitats, such as dense forests, grasslands, swamps, and even deserts. They tend to live where there is plenty of water, either near rivers or streams or in swampland. Jaguars can live as far north as the southern United States. Today they are mostly found in remote parts of Central and South America, ranging from Mexico to the north of Argentina. The biggest population of jaguars lives in the vast Amazon rainforest.

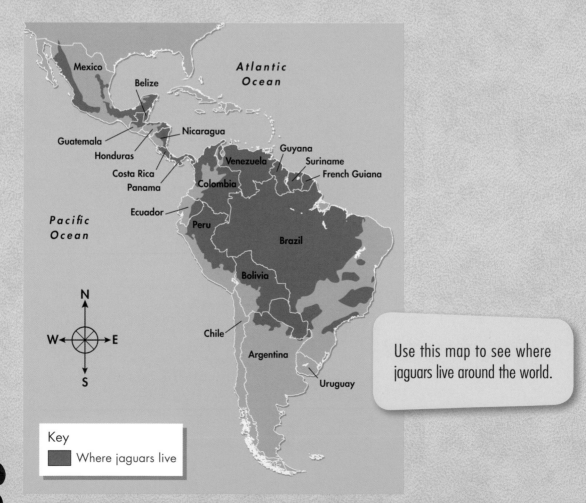

Use this map to see where jaguars live around the world.

Key
▭ Where jaguars live

A perfect jaguar habitat has plenty of water, thick vegetation, and lots of animals to hunt.

A place to hunt

Jaguars live in habitats where they are able to hunt and kill plenty of prey. When jaguars hunt, they stay on the ground and like to have plenty of cover from plants and trees to help them stalk prey unseen. They also like to climb into trees to locate prey or hide.

HIDDEN CAMERAS

Scientists in Arizona, USA, have set up cameras in a mountainous region that have captured recent photographs of jaguars. Jaguars used to live in New Mexico and Texas, as well as Arizona, but during the 20th century these populations disappeared. Now it is thought that a few cats have moved back to Arizona from Mexico. Scientists hope that these cats might **mate** and the population could grow again.

What adaptations help jaguars survive?

Animals have adaptations that help them to survive in their particular habitat in a particular way. These adaptations develop in a species over thousands of years. Jaguars are adapted to be able to hunt prey successfully in the habitats where they live.

Camouflage

The rosette patterns on a jaguar's fur are an important adaptation for this stealthy predator. Hiding is important because a jaguar hunts its prey by stalking and ambushing rather than chasing over long distances. On the forest floor, the dappled light shining down through the trees blends in perfectly with the pattern on a jaguar's coat, helping to camouflage it. In more open terrain, the pattern also acts as camouflage by breaking up the animal's outline. Jaguars with black fur are well camouflaged in dark, shadowy places.

Jaguars need to stay hidden for as long as possible to get close to prey animals.

Swimming

Unlike many other cats, jaguars are adapted to be able to swim very well. Their strong, sturdy legs and large paws enable them to do this. These adaptations give the jaguar more choice of prey, as it is able to hunt for turtles, fish, and caiman in rivers as well as stalking animals on land.

HUNTED

Like many other big cats, in the past the jaguar was hunted for its beautiful coat. During the 20th century, as many as 18,000 jaguars were killed every year to make fur coats and other goods for humans. In 1973, this fur trade was virtually stopped and selling parts of a jaguar's body is now against the law.

Jaguars can climb trees while hunting prey or looking for a place to rest.

Night vision

Like many other cats, jaguars have eyes that are well adapted to hunting for prey at night. Many animals that have good night vision have a structure at the back of their eyes called the tapetum lucidum that acts like a mirror. This reflects any light, giving the animal much clearer vision than an animal without this adaptation. Jaguars have this special eye adaptation. A jaguar's eyes are positioned at the front of its face, giving it **binocular vision**. This enables them to judge distances well, which helps them decide when to leap out at prey.

Other senses

A jaguar's sense of hearing is also adapted to help it locate prey. Its small, rounded ears are very sensitive and can turn in the direction of any noise they pick up. This helps the jaguar to assess where prey is very accurately. They can even turn their ears in separate directions at the same time.

A jaguar's sense of smell is well developed but it tends to use this to find other jaguars to mate with rather than to track prey.

WHISKERS

Jaguars have a set of sensitive whiskers around their face and head, with most around their mouth. These whiskers are called vibrissae and work by gathering information from the movement of air near the jaguar, telling the hunter if prey is nearby. A jaguar relies especially on its vibrissae when hunting in the dark. Its whiskers are also **tactile**, playing an important part in the jaguar's sense of touch.

A jaguar's eyes are positioned at the front of its face. This is one feature that helps make them excellent hunters.

Jaguar jaws are the strongest of all the cats.

Killer jaws

A jaguar's stocky head contains a set of large, powerful jaws. The jaguar's huge jaw muscles define the shape of its face. This adaptation enables the jaguar to hunt and kill almost any other animal in its environment. A predator with such powerful jaws has no problem crunching through the skull of its prey after it has leapt in for the kill.

The huge canine teeth inside the jaguar's mouth help it to grip hold of struggling prey and to tear flesh from its victims as it feeds. The jaguar is the only cat that uses its canine teeth to bite between its prey's ears and pierce its brain to kill it.

Strong body

Jaguars also have powerful, muscular bodies. They need this strength to hold down prey and to drag it to a better location to feed on once killed. A jaguar's stocky legs and body make it easier for the cat to creep low to the ground as it stalks its victims. Its short, muscular legs enable it to leap from a standstill, while its strong front paws are useful for climbing trees.

MOVING JAGUARS

Jaguars as we know them today have been around for between 280,000 and 510,000 years. They used to live much further north, but scientists believe they moved south as the climate became colder. Having made their home in warmer climates, the jaguar then developed various adaptations over time that suited their new home.

Jaguars can even crack open the tough shells of turtles with their powerful jaws.

What do jaguars eat?

Jaguars are carnivores and only eat meat. Because jaguars live in a range of different habitats, their diet can vary considerably from place to place. Like many other cats, jaguars are **opportunistic** hunters, which means they will eat many different types of animals should they come across them. Eating a wide range of species is very useful, because if one type of animal is affected by changes in the environment, there should still be plenty of other prey animals left for the jaguar to eat.

Varied diet

Scientists studying jaguars in the wild have counted more than 85 species eaten by them. The animals they tend to eat most often include capybara, a large mammal that looks a bit like a big guinea pig, and peccary, a pig-like mammal. Other common prey are birds, deer, armadillos, tapirs, and domestic cattle. Jaguars will also hunt for food in water, so their diet includes fish, turtles, and caiman, an alligator-like reptile.

Capybaras live in groups and spend a lot of time in water.

This jaguar is struggling to overpower a caiman.

Hunting

Jaguars creep up close to prey before leaping out and surprising it. The jaguar then makes a swift kill by biting through the victim's skull or clamping its jaws around its prey's throat to suffocate it. It can kill smaller prey with one swipe of a front paw. Jaguars can also leap into water to catch prey. They are strong swimmers, so can carry prey back to the shore before eating.

JAGUAR ATTACKS

Jaguars do not normally attack humans. They tend to keep out of people's way and will only hurt humans if they are cornered or wounded. Unfortunately, in many places where jaguars live people are afraid of them and may shoot the cats to avoid attack.

19

Feeding

A jaguar tends to eat large prey starting at the head, eating the tongue, and then eating the internal organs. When eating a turtle, the jaguar will either break open the shell with its teeth and jaws or scoop out the turtle's soft body from under the shell with its paw. Jaguars need to eat at least 1.4 kilograms (3.1 pounds) of meat each day on average to get the energy they need.

Jaguar food web

All animals have to eat plants or other animals to live and they, in turn, may be eaten by other animals. This is called a **food chain**. The energy in a food chain starts with the sun. Plants use the sun's energy to make food and are called **producers**. Animals are called **consumers** because they consume (eat) plants or other animals. Animals that eat plants for energy make up the next link in the food chain. These include many of the animals eaten by jaguars. Carnivores make up the next link in the food chain, getting their energy from the animals they eat. Many connected food chains make up a **food web**.

Jaguars can eat extra meat when they kill large prey and then go several days without eating.

CARLOS A. LOPEZ GONZALEZ

Carlos A. Lopez Gonzalez is a Mexican scientist who has studied jaguars in the wild. He has observed jaguars to monitor whether prey of a certain size was important in their diet. His research concluded that jaguars don't depend on large prey, such as peccaries, but survive just as well on a diet of medium-sized prey.

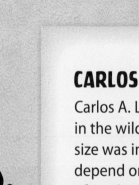

This is a food web. The arrows go from the plant or animal being eaten to the animal that eats it. In this food web capybaras, peccaries, and fish eat plants. Jaguars eat capybaras, peccaries, and fish. They also eat the caiman that eat the fish.

Jaguar

Caiman

Capybara

Fish

Peccary

Rainforest plants

River plants

What is a jaguar's life cycle?

An animal's life cycle is the stages it goes through from birth to death. A jaguar's life cycle goes through three main stages: birth, youth, and adulthood. Jaguars reach adulthood when they are old enough to **reproduce** and have cubs themselves.

Meeting and mating

Adult jaguars usually live and hunt alone, apart from mothers caring for cubs. Jaguars can mate at any time of year but the best time to have cubs is during the rainy season as there is much more prey around. Female jaguars are normally about two to three years old when they mate, while males tend to be three to four years old. The females attract a mate by making special sounds at certain times of day and **scent-marking** their territory. Once they have mated, the male and female separate and live alone once more.

Adult male and female jaguars only spend time together when it is time to mate.

A newborn jaguar cub weighs about 8 times as much as a newborn pet kitten.

Birth of cubs

A female jaguar is **pregnant** for about 100 days. She finds a safe and sheltered place to give birth, in a den located in a cave or under a fallen tree trunk. She can give birth to between one and four cubs, but usually has two. Newborn cubs weigh about 820 grams (28.9 ounces).

RAINFOREST SEASONS

The jaguar mostly lives in tropical regions, which have two seasons: a rainy season and a dry season. The rainy season lasts for several months, with heavy rainfall and hot, humid weather. During this season, there is an increase in plant growth, making more food at the start of the food chain.

Cub development

Jaguar cubs are born with their eyes closed. They only open them after around two weeks. They are completely dependent on their mother, feeding on milk produced by her and staying safe in the den for several months. They are able to start walking after about 18 days. Cubs start to eat meat as well as drinking milk after about three months. Initially, this meat is brought to the den by their mother. Cubs continue to drink milk until they are about six months old.

Jaguar cubs learn to play with each other and their mother when they are small.

Staying safe

Mother jaguars are very protective of their cubs. Young jaguars could be attacked by harpy eagles or by adult males that kill them off to reduce competition. This is why the cubs stay safe in their den until they are old and strong enough to run away from danger and learn from their mother.

SPECIAL CUBS

In November 2012, two jaguar cubs were born at the Milwaukee County Zoo in Wisconsin, USA. Conservationists think these cubs are extra special because their father was born in the wild. He was killing cattle and so was taken into captivity for his own safety, bringing new genes into the population of captive jaguars. Both cubs are male and so will be much needed when they mature to mate with the mainly female population of jaguars in zoos. Breeding programmes in zoos and other institutions are important for keeping up the numbers of species that are endangered in the wild.

Rosewaine
Learning Centra

Learning to hunt

When jaguar cubs are around six months old, they are old enough to leave the den and go out hunting with their mother. This is important as they gradually learn how to hunt by watching her. Playing and wrestling with siblings and their mother is also an important part of learning to hunt for a predator.

Independence

Jaguar cubs leave their mother at around two years of age but they may keep in touch from time to time for several months after this. When the cubs reach the age of three or four years, they are ready to mate themselves and the cycle will begin again.

A jaguar cub stays close to its mother until it is old enough to survive on its own.

Cat	Lifespan in the wild
Cheetah	around 12 years
Lion	around 15 years
Jaguar	around 15 years
Leopard	around 15 years
Puma	around 20 years
Tiger	around 20 years

This chart shows the lifespan of some big cats in the wild.

How do jaguars behave?

Jaguars tend to live alone, except when mating or raising cubs. Like many other predators, jaguars are **territorial**. This means they mark out their own area of land, called a **home range**, and defend it against other jaguars. Doing this ensures there is enough prey available for them to hunt and eat when they need to.

A female jaguar needs to be able to hunt over an area of about 25–38 square kilometres (9.5–14.6 square miles), while males need two or three times as much space. Two or three females might have their home ranges within one male's home range. Some home ranges have been observed to be over 250 square kilometres (96 square miles). Jaguars will spend a lot of time travelling within their home range every day.

Defending territory

Male jaguars can defend their home ranges in two ways: by fighting other males that intrude and by marking their space. However, scientists studying jaguars in Brazil have observed that male jaguars there were not particularly aggressive towards other males entering their home range. They are more likely to mark their home range by making noises, scratching bark off trees at the borders of their territory, scraping the ground with their back feet, and by scent marking plants using **urine** and **faeces**.

WILD SECRETS

It's difficult for scientists to gather information about jaguars' behaviour in the wild, as they tend to live in remote habitats with dense vegetation. Knowledge about jaguars' behaviour has mainly been pieced together by putting radio or GPS collars on cats, studying photographs taken by **camera traps**, and observing the presence of tracks and kills.

Scratching bark off trees is one way male jaguars mark their home range.

Hunting and resting

Radio collars fitted to jaguars have shown scientists that jaguars can be active at any time of day or night, probably depending on the activity of prey where they live. Like many other big cats, their preferred time for hunting is early morning and early evening. This behaviour is known as **crepuscular**. When the day is particularly hot, from mid-morning until mid-afternoon, jaguars tend to rest. They find a secluded spot deep in the shade, for example under rocks, inside caves, or under leafy plants and trees. Sometimes they climb trees to rest on a strong branch.

Strong swimmers

Jaguars love water and will often stay close to it as they move around. In the Amazon rainforest, jaguars rarely stray further than half a kilometre from water. They enjoy swimming and can use rivers to travel to islands where prey might be found. Jaguars swim with their head and back above the waterline and will even play in the water as cubs.

JAGUAR CAMP

The Jaguar Research Center is located in the Pantanal tropical-wetland region in Brazil and provides a unique opportunity for people to observe jaguar behaviour. Visitors can stay at the camp and are almost guaranteed a sighting of jaguars, as so many live in that particular area. They can be seen catching prey in the river and resting in the shade. Most scientific observations of wild jaguar behaviour have been made here.

Jaguars use water to cool
off when temperatures
become very hot.

A DAY IN THE LIFE OF A JAGUAR

A jaguar's day consists of sleeping, resting, and hunting. A female jaguar in the wild might sleep from midnight until around 3.00 a.m. She would then wake up and start to roam around her territory, hunting for prey. After making a kill in the early morning, she will take her victim to a safe place to feed herself. Then she takes some meat back to her cubs in their den and also feeds them with milk.

During the hottest part of the day, a female jaguar often rests in the shade with her cubs, **grooming** them by licking their fur with her long tongue. She will also spend a lot of time grooming herself, particularly her forelegs and paws. Cubs enjoy playing and wrestling with each other and their mother. The family might visit the river to cool down and play some more. The mother jaguar makes sure she gets her cubs back to the safety of the den or to a new den if she senses a male jaguar is nearby.

As dusk falls, jaguars that have not already hunted that day will search for prey before stalking it and killing it. As night draws in, they will sleep again, either in their den with cubs or in a high place, such as up a tree or on a rock.

LEANDRO SILVEIRA AND ANAH JACOMO

Leandro Silveira and Anah Jacomo are Brazilian biologists who cared for three jaguar cubs after their mother was shot by cattle ranchers. Leandro and Anah taught the cubs how to hunt, climb trees, and swim so that eventually they might be able to survive in the wild. After two years, the scientists tried to release the jaguars, but when the cats roamed close to farmland they had to be taken back into captivity for their own safety.

It's important for jaguars and other big cats to rest during the day to save energy for hunting.

How intelligent are jaguars?

It is difficult to identify and measure what we know as intelligence in animals. Much of the way they behave is based on **instinct** as much as intelligence. However, jaguars seem to demonstrate intelligent behaviour in several ways that are crucial to their survival.

Communication

The way animals communicate tells us a lot about their intelligence. Jaguars communicate in a variety of ways, mainly using sounds and smell. Jaguars can make a range of noises, including roaring, which is mainly used to warn intruders to leave another cat's territory. They make a grunting sound that is a bit like a cough to communicate with other jaguars over a long distance or to mark out their territory. Jaguars can also make a snorting, or chuffing, noise that is known as prusten. This is a friendly noise that is similar to the purring sound made by other cats. Tigers, snow leopards, and clouded leopards can also make this noise. Jaguars use prusten when they are relaxed and contented.

Jaguars are also able to use their sense of smell to interpret markings left by other jaguars. These include scraped up earth, urine sprayed into bushes, and faeces left in prominent places. These markings tell them if they are entering another jaguar's home range.

A jaguar's roar sounds like a deep, loud cough.

JAGUAR TALES

Stories told by South American Indians have described jaguars that dip their tails into rivers to lure fish to the surface so they can catch them. If this were true, it would mean jaguars are able to use a 'tool' (their tail) to help them catch prey. However, there is no evidence to prove this behaviour, so we can't be sure that it really happens.

What threats do jaguars face?

Jaguars face a number of threats which have led to them becoming a species in danger. The Convention of International Trade in Endangered Species (CITES) is an organization that registers animal population numbers to alert governments, conservationists, and the public if a species is decreasing in numbers. CITES has classified jaguars as 'near threatened'.

Loss of habitat

A major threat to jaguars is loss of their habitat, mainly due to forest being cut down by humans to use the land for farming and the wood for building. Jaguars need to be able to roam over long distances within a region ranging from Mexico to Argentina, but human development often stops them from moving where they want to go and makes it difficult for them to find a mate.

This map shows the past and present ranges of the jaguar.

Humans have cut down large areas of forest in South America to use the wood and also for cattle farming.

Loss of prey

Although jaguars will hunt a wide range of prey animals, it is becoming harder for them to hunt. There is less prey available in the reduced space left for them after habitat destruction. Humans also hunt the jaguars' typical prey, leaving fewer animals for the cats to feed on.

Human threat

The expansion of the human population is one of the biggest threats to jaguars and many other wild animals. When jaguars move into areas where people live and farm to search for prey, they are likely to kill farm animals, which makes them very unpopular. Very often jaguars are shot by ranchers, who see jaguars as a threat to their livestock. If a mother with cubs is shot, the young jaguars usually die too.

How can people help jaguars?

Many people and organizations are working hard to help protect jaguars. This beautiful, mysterious animal appeals to many visitors in zoos and wildlife parks around the world. In zoos, endangered species such as the jaguar can be studied, so we are able to learn more about their needs and behaviour. Captive jaguars can also take part in breeding programmes that help to boost population numbers. Visitors to zoos and wildlife parks learn about these stunning creatures and are more likely to support any efforts to protect them in the wild.

JAGUAR HUNTING

The fur trade used to be responsible for the deaths of thousands of jaguars each year. This trade has now been made illegal, but jaguars are still shot by people who either ignore laws protecting the animals or have permission to kill the cats. Animals that cause a problem to farmers can still be hunted in Brazil, Peru, Costa Rica, Guatemala, and Mexico. In Bolivia, hunters can get permission to kill jaguars as **trophies**, and in Ecuador and Guyana jaguars are completely unprotected. Jaguars are now extinct in El Salvador and Uruguay.

This scientist has put a radio collar on a jaguar so its movements can be followed.

Protected areas

In order for populations to increase, jaguars need to live in special areas where they are not under threat from humans. In Belize, a wildlife preserve has been set up to protect jaguars. Around 200 jaguars live on the 150 square kilometres (58 square miles) of rainforest that makes up the reserve. In Brazil, a special centre is to be set up to focus on the conservation of predators such as the jaguar and to work with farmers and other people who can come into conflict with the cats.

Conservation groups

As well as governments in Central and South America, conservation organizations are working hard to protect jaguars. These include the World Wildlife Foundation, Panthera, and the Jaguar Conservation Fund. They raise awareness about these and other endangered animals and raise money to help protect them.

Panthera has taken a leading role in jaguar conservation. It was involved in setting up the Jaguar Preserve in Belize and is currently involved in the Jaguar Corridor Initiative (JCI). This initiative involves 13 of the 18 countries where jaguars live. Because there are no subspecies of jaguar, this big cat is the same wherever it lives. It is the only large carnivore of this type in the world that moves over long distances, so the JCI is an attempt to create a 'corridor', linking jaguars from Argentina to Mexico. This will allow the animals to roam as far and as freely as they need to. Working with governments and other charities, the JCI works with local communities to help them live alongside jaguars and farm cattle without coming into conflict with the cats.

Eco-tourism

People who live in areas where jaguars are found can benefit from the income brought by eco-tourism. This involves visitors staying locally in order to visit the jaguar's habitat and see them in the wild. The benefits of eco-tourism act as incentive for humans who share space with jaguars to help protect them.

These jaguar cubs were born at a zoo in Mexico in 2012.

DR ALAN RABINOWITZ

Dr Alan Rabinowitz is CEO of Panthera and a big cat expert. During the 1980s, he was involved in the first radio-collaring of jaguars in Belize and went on to play an important role in the setting up of the country's jaguar preserve. The Jaguar Corridor Initiative is one of Dr Rabinowitz's greatest achievements. He has also worked on a similar corridor initiative for tigers in the Himalayas.

What does the future hold for jaguars?

The jaguar isn't as endangered as many of the world's other big cats, but it still remains 'near threatened'. Although laws have been passed to protect this magnificent cat, unless they are enforced effectively, jaguar numbers will continue to fall as they are killed in great numbers or lose more of their habitat.

Governments need to ban jaguar hunting altogether and focus on educating the people who live alongside jaguars to help them understand what a valuable species it is. If the jaguar is protected and able to flourish, then many other species that share its habitat will be protected too.

Positive steps

Activities to protect jaguars, such as the Brazilian government's National Center for Research, Management, and Conservation of Predators and the Jaguar Corridor Initiative, should go a long way towards addressing the threats jaguars face. If everyone is committed to understanding and helping jaguars, then we can hope that they have a future in the wild.

JAGUAR PROTECTION

The Wildlife Conservation Society (WCS) began a jaguar conservation programme in 1999, focusing on scientific research into jaguars' needs. They work to protect jaguars in areas where their populations are dwindling, showing farmers that using guard dogs can protect their livestock from jaguars so they don't need to shoot them. They also look at environmentally friendly ways to keep jaguars away from human settlements and reduce pollution that can harm the cats.

This jaguar lives in a zoo in Belize.

Jaguar profile

Species:	Jaguar
Latin name:	*Panthera onca*
Length:	1.2 metres (4 feet)
Weight:	100–160 kilograms (220–350 pounds)
Tail length:	60–90 centimetres (2–3 feet)
Habitat:	Dense forests, grasslands, swamps, and deserts in Central and South America
Diet:	Capybara, peccary, birds, deer, armadillo, tapir, domestic cattle, fish, turtles, and caiman, among other animals
Number of cubs per litter:	Around one to four cubs, with two on average. Females are around two to three years old when they are ready to have cubs and give birth about once every two or three years.
Life expectancy:	Up to 15 years

The spotted coat provides good camouflage for hunting.

Large eyes are able to see well in the dark and judge distances accurately.

Short, strong back legs help the jaguar creep close to the forest floor when hunting.

Large front paws can kill small prey with one swipe. They also help the jaguar to swim.

Powerful jaws can pierce a skull or a turtle's shell.

Glossary

adaptation body part or behaviour of a living thing that helps it survive in a particular habitat

apex predator animal that hunts other animals for food and is not hunted by any other animals for food

binocular vision using both eyes together to see

camera trap hidden camera that takes pictures of animals in the wild

camouflage blending in with the environment to hide

classify group living things together by their similarities and differences

consumer animal that eats plants or other animals

crepuscular active in the early morning and early evening

faeces poo

food chain sequence in which one creature eats another, which eats another, and so on

food web network of intertwined food chains

genes characteristics passed on from a parent to offspring

groom clean an animal's fur

habitat type of place or surroundings that a living thing prefers to live in

home range area in which an animal usually lives

instinct natural tendency or way of behaving

litter group of young animals born at the same time

mate come together to reproduce or have young

melanistic condition where animals have black fur rather than typical colouring

opportunistic able to hunt and kill whatever prey is available

pregnant condition where a female animal is carrying developing young in her body

prey animal that is hunted and killed for food by another animal

producer plant in a food chain that makes food

reproduce to have offspring

rosette spotted pattern on a jaguar's fur

scent-marking marking territory using smell

species group of similar living things that can mate with each other

tactile to do with the sense of touch

territorial when an animal claims an area of land as its own space

trophy something to show an achievement, for example some hunters kill animals to show their skill

urine liquid waste from an animal

Find out more

Books

Countdown to Extinction, David Burnie (Oxford University Press, 2008)

South America's Most Amazing Animals (Animal Top Tens), Anita Ganeri (Raintree, 2009)

ZSL Big Cats, Michael Cox (Bloomsbury Childrens, 2012)

Websites

BBC Nature
www.bbc.co.uk/nature/life/Jaguar
Visit this website to watch videos of jaguars in the wild.

The Jaguar Conservation Fund
www.jaguar.org.br/en/index.html
Visit this website to see what work is being done to protect jaguars in Brazil.

Organizations

The World Wildlife Fund
www.wwf.org.uk
WWF works to protect animals and nature, and needs your help!
Take a look at their website and see what you can do.

The Born Free Foundation
www.bornfree.org
This charity works to protect jaguars and many other endangered wild animals.

Panthera
www.panthera.org
This leading charity works to protect jaguars and other big cats.
Find out more about their work on their website.

Index